W9-ACC-716

TODAY'S 12 HOTTEST
MUSIC SUPERSTARS

by Annabelle Tometich

www.12StoryLibrary.com

12-Story Library is an imprint of Peterson Publishing Company and Press Room Editions.

Produced for 12-Story Library by Red Line Editorial

Photographs ©: Chris Pizzello/Invision/AP Images, cover, 1, 11; Jason Merritt/Thinkstock, 4; Everett Collection/Shutterstock Images, 5; Debby Wong/Shutterstock Images, 6; Jaguar PS/Shutterstock Images, 7; Andre Durao/Shutterstock Images, 8, 17; Helga Esteb/Shutterstock Images, 9, 26, 28; Matt Sayles/Invision/AP Images, 12; Featureflash/Shutterstock Images, 14, 23, 25; Julio Cortez/AP Images, 15; Northfoto/Shutterstock Images, 18; Shutterstock Images, 19; S Bukley/Shutterstock Images, 20; Erika Goldring/Thinkstock, 21, 29; Antonio Scorza/Shutterstock Images, 24; Frederick M. Brown/Thinkstock, 27

ISBN
978-1-63235-020-6 (hardcover)
978-1-63235-080-0 (paperback)
978-1-62143-061-2 (hosted ebook)

Library of Congress Control Number: 2014946797

Printed in the United States of America
Mankato, MN
October, 2014

Go beyond the book. Get free, up-to-date content on this topic at 12StoryLibrary.com.

TABLE OF CONTENTS

BEYONCÉ BREAKS OFF ON HER OWN

Beyoncé grew up performing. As a child, she sang for tips in her mother's hair salon. When she wasn't singing, she swept up hair from the floor.

Beyoncé formed the group Destiny's Child in 1997 with her cousin and two classmates. Beyoncé was the lead singer. She had a powerful voice. She loved to dance. Beyoncé started her solo career in 2003.

Beyoncé has recorded five albums. She has also starred in several movies. Beyoncé married rapper Jay-Z, also known as Shawn Carter, in 2008. The couple has worked and sung together for many of their songs. Beyoncé gave birth to their daughter, Blue Ivy Carter, on January 7, 2012.

Beyoncé poses with her Grammy for Best Traditional R&B Performance for "Love on Top" in 2013.

11 million

Number of copies *Dangerously in Love* sold.

Full Name: Beyoncé Giselle Knowles-Carter

Birth Date: September 4, 1981

Birthplace: Houston, Texas

Breakthrough Moment: In 2003, Beyoncé's first solo album *Dangerously in Love* won five Grammy Awards.

Awards: 17 Grammy Awards, the third-most for a female artist

BEYONCÉ

On December 13, 2013, Beyoncé released a surprise album titled *Beyoncé*. She released the album without any advertising. She didn't even tell her fans. *Beyoncé* sold an amazing 828,773 copies in just three days. Beyoncé's one-year-old daughter, Blue Ivy, sings with her on the song "Blue."

After rising to fame with Destiny's Child bandmates Kelly Rowland (left) and Michelle Williams (right), Beyoncé began her own career.

2

MILEY CYRUS: FROM HANNAH MONTANA TO MUSIC SUPERSTAR

Miley Cyrus grew up on her family's farm in Tennessee. As a baby, she smiled all the time. Her family nicknamed her "Smiley Miley."

Cyrus performs on NBC's *Today Show* in New York City in 2013.

Cyrus loved performing even as a child. She starred and sang in plays at school. Cyrus was confident and funny. In 2004, she beat out more than 1,000 other young actresses for the role of Hannah Montana. *Hannah Montana* was a show on the Disney Channel. It was about a teen girl who lived a secret life as a music superstar. By 2006,

Cyrus was a superstar of her own. She has starred in movies. She has four music albums.

Cyrus cut her hair short in 2012. She wanted to break away from her old Hannah Montana character. Cyrus is known for her low, raspy voice. She is famous for edgy performances.

11
Miley Cyrus's age when she auditioned for *Hannah Montana*.

Birth Name: Destiny Hope Cyrus

Birth Date: November 23, 1992

Birthplace: Franklin, Tennessee

Breakthrough Moment: In 2005, Cyrus landed the lead role in the Disney TV show *Hannah Montana*.

Awards: 1 MTV Movie Award, 6 Teen Choice Awards, 1 People's Choice Award

MILEY'S FAMOUS FATHER

Miley Cyrus is the daughter of Billy Ray Cyrus. Billy Ray was a country singer. He is famous for his 1992 song "Achy Breaky Heart." Miley and her dad often work together. Billy Ray played Miley's father on *Hannah Montana*. They sang together on the 2007 song "Ready, Set, Don't Go." The song was featured on one of Billy Ray's albums.

Cyrus stands with her father, Billy Ray Cyrus, at the premier of *Hannah Montana The Movie* in 2009.

ADAM LEVINE: MAROON 5'S LEADING MAN

Adam Levine started his first band as a teenager. The band was called Kara's Flowers. It featured Levine and three of his classmates. The band first performed at a school dance. Levine was so shy he played guitar with his back to the audience.

Levine studied music at a performing arts college in New York. He learned different styles, such as R&B and hip-hop. He eventually moved

Levine performs in concert with his band, Maroon 5, in Brazil in 2011.

Levine stands with Carson Daly (left) and other judges of *The Voice*, CeeLo Green (middle), Christina Aguilera (second from right), and Blake Shelton (right).

back to California and started the band Maroon 5.

Maroon 5 won the 2004 Grammy Award for Best New Artist. Levine writes many of their songs. He is known for his smooth voice. He can sing a wide range of notes. In 2011, Levine became a singing judge and coach on the TV show *The Voice*.

10 million
Number of copies
Songs About Jane sold.

Full Name: Adam Noah Levine

Birth Date: March 18, 1979

Birthplace: Los Angeles, California

Breakthrough Moment: In 2004, Maroon 5's album *Songs About Jane* went platinum.

Awards: 3 Grammy Awards with Maroon 5

LORDE WINS TWO GRAMMY AWARDS BY AGE 17

Lorde's mother is a prize-winning poet. She taught Lorde to love reading and writing. At the age of five, Lorde joined a drama group. She found that she also loved singing. In 2009, Lorde sang in her school's talent show. A friend's father sent her performance to record companies. Lorde signed a record deal when she was 13.

Lorde became the first New Zealand artist to have a number one hit in the United States. "Royals" had more than 4.4 million downloads in the United States in 2013.

Lorde chose her nickname because of her obsession with royalty. She is known for her gothic style and dark lipstick. In 2014, Lorde won two Grammy Awards. She was only 17.

2
Number of winners in Grammy history younger than Lorde when she won for "Royals" at age 17.

Birth Name: Ella Marija Lani Yelich-O'Connor

Birth Date: November 7, 1996

Birthplace: Takapuna, Auckland, New Zealand

Breakthrough Moment: Lorde's single "Royals" was ranked number one on the *Billboard* Hot 100 for nine weeks in 2013.

Awards: 2 Grammy Awards

Lorde gives a speech after winning an award for Top New Artist at the *Billboard* Music Awards in 2014.

5

MACKLEMORE WINS BEST NEW ARTIST GRAMMY

Macklemore grew up in Seattle. His mother was a social worker. She taught him to appreciate people's differences. The rapper released his first album in 2005 under the name Professor Macklemore. He chose the nickname because of the crazy outfits he bought at thrift

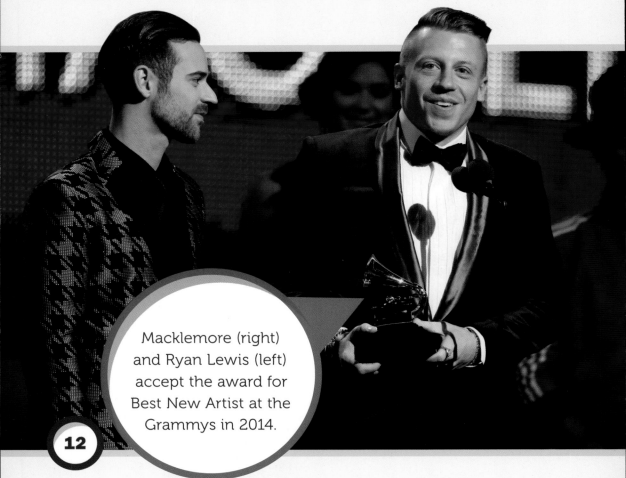

Macklemore (right) and Ryan Lewis (left) accept the award for Best New Artist at the Grammys in 2014.

12

33

Number of couples who were married while Macklemore performed "Same Love" at the 2014 Grammy Awards ceremony.

Birth Name: Ben Haggerty

Birth Date: June 19, 1983

Birthplace: Seattle, Washington

Breakthrough Moment: In 2010, Macklemore and Ryan Lewis's song "Thrift Shop" was downloaded more than 6 million times.

Awards: 4 Grammy Awards, 2 American Music Awards

SINGING FOR ACCEPTANCE

Macklemore raps about his gay uncle in his songs. He uses his music to promote tolerance. He wants people of all lifestyles to feel accepted. At the 2014 Grammy Awards, Macklemore and Ryan Lewis performed "Same Love." They sang the song for newlywed couples, both gay and straight.

shops. He dropped the Professor part. But his friends kept calling him Macklemore.

In 2006, Macklemore met Ryan Lewis through the social media website Myspace. Ryan was a DJ from Spokane, Washington. Ryan

and Macklemore liked each other's musical styles. In 2012, they release their first album *The Heist*. It featured the hit songs "Thrift Shop" and "Same Love."

The album was unlike many hip-hop albums of the time. Macklemore rapped about gay rights. He made it cool to shop at Goodwill and other thrift stores. Macklemore and Ryan Lewis won four Grammys in 2014.

BRUNO MARS TAKES THE STAGE AT THE SUPER BOWL

Bruno Mars grew up in a musical family. His father played drums. His mother was a singer. The family nicknamed him "Bruno" when he was a baby. He was independent and strong. His sister said he was kind of a brute.

Mars's family performed in shows in Hawaii. They played covers of famous songs. When Mars was four years old, he joined the family's act. He played the part of Elvis Presley. He later impersonated Michael Jackson. Mars became a young star.

Mars taught himself to play the drums, guitar, and piano. He moved to Los Angeles, California,

In 2011, Mars won an American Music Award for Favorite Pop/Rock Male Artist.

in 2002.
He began
writing songs for
other musicians.

Mars began writing songs for himself. He has sold more than 130 million singles worldwide. Mars won his first Grammy in 2010.

Mars put on a lively halftime performance for Super Bowl XLVIII in 2014.

18

Number of Grammy nominations for Mars through 2013.

Birth Name: Peter Gene Hernandez

Birth Date: October 8, 1985

Birthplace: Honolulu, Hawaii

Breakthrough Moment: In 2010, Mars's song "Nothin' on You" with rapper B.o.B. hit number one on *Billboard*'s singles chart.

Awards: 2 Grammy Awards, 1 American Music Award

SUPER BOWL PERFORMER

In February 2014, Mars received a rare opportunity. He performed during the halftime show of the Super Bowl. Nearly 100 million people watched. Mars's brother played drums for him. Mars's voice and stage presence impressed the critics.

KATY PERRY: CONSERVATIVE TO COLORFUL

Katy Perry grew up in a conservative family. Her mother and father were pastors. They didn't let Katy listen to rock or pop music. Katy took singing lessons when she was nine years old. She recorded a gospel album in 2001. It did not sell well. But Katy didn't want to give up.

Perry moved to Los Angeles, California, when she was 17. She struggled to make a living. She once sold some of her clothes to pay for a place to live. Perry decided to use her mother's maiden name of Perry. Several of her record deals failed. But Perry kept going. In 2008, she earned a Grammy nomination for her hit "I Kissed a Girl."

Perry became known for wearing colorful outfits and wigs. Her second album *Teenage Dream* produced five number one singles. Her third album *Prism* released in 2013. It featured the smash single "Roar."

69
Number of consecutive weeks Perry spent in the top 10 of the *Billboard* Hot 100, making her the first female artist to achieve that feat.

Birth Name: Katheryn Elizabeth Hudson

Birth Date: October 25, 1984

Birthplace: Santa Barbara, California

Breakthrough Moment: Perry's single "I Kissed a Girl" topped the charts in 2008.

Awards: 2 American Music Awards, 6 *Billboard* Music Awards

Perry wears a colorful costume while performing live in Brazil in 2011.

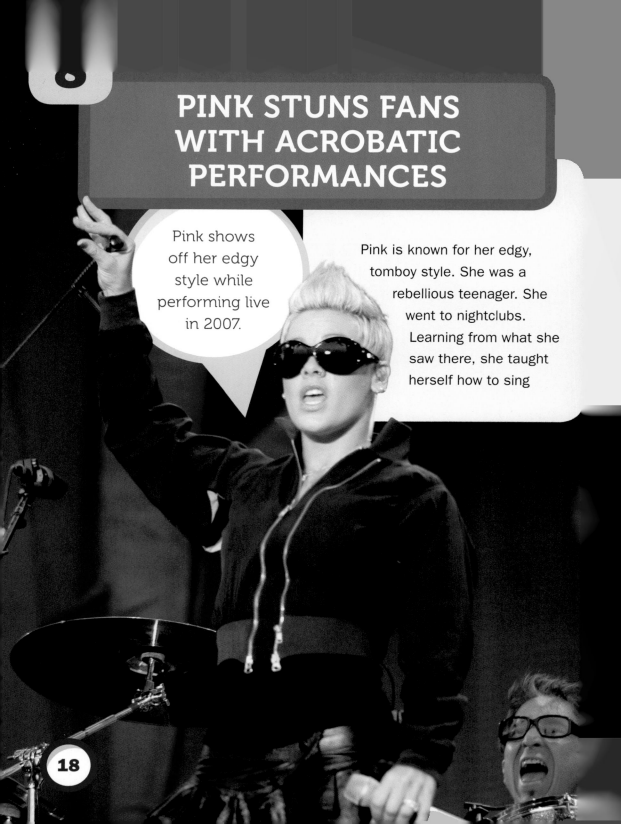

PINK STUNS FANS WITH ACROBATIC PERFORMANCES

Pink shows off her edgy style while performing live in 2007.

Pink is known for her edgy, tomboy style. She was a rebellious teenager. She went to nightclubs. Learning from what she saw there, she taught herself how to sing

Pink is known for her strong body and acrobatic performances.

and dance. At age 14, she started writing music.

Pink dropped out of high school. She had a knack for finding trouble. But no one could deny she had a talent for music. She changed her name from Alecia to Pink. She got the nickname from a character in a movie she liked.

In 2000, Pink released her first solo album. She wanted to be more than a pretty face. Pink now has seven albums. She's become known for her strong voice and body. Pink performed acrobatic feats at the 2010 and 2014 Grammy Awards. She flew above the stage on ribbons and wires as she sang. She trains often to stay in shape for her shows.

7

Peak position on the *Billboard* Hot 100 of Pink's first single, "There You Go" in 2000.

Birth Name: Alecia Beth Moore

Birth Date: September 8, 1979

Birthplace: Doylestown, Pennsylvania

Breakthrough Moment: Pink's first solo album *Can't Take Me Home* went platinum in 2000.

Awards: 3 Grammy Awards, 5 *Billboard* Music Awards

BLAKE SHELTON GOES PLATINUM

Blake Shelton started singing and performing at a young age. When he was 16, he won an award for best young entertainer in Oklahoma. Shelton graduated high school in 1994. Two weeks later, he moved to Nashville, Tennessee. He started out as a songwriter.

Then Shelton began singing his own songs. He released a string of successful albums from 2004 to 2009. Shelton is known for his laid-back style. He has a smooth voice and a Southern twang.

In 2011, Shelton married Miranda Lambert. She is also a country singer. That same year he became a judge on the hit TV show *The Voice.* The show exposed Shelton to a new audience. Shelton's career took off.

Shelton performs at the JCPenney Holiday Giving Tour in 2012.

5

Number of weeks "Austin," Shelton's first single, spent at number one on the *Billboard* Hot Country Songs chart in 2001.

Full Name: Blake Tollison Shelton

Birth Date: June 18, 1976

Birthplace: Ada, Oklahoma

Breakthrough Moment: In 2002, Shelton's debut album *Blake Shelton* went gold.

Awards: 1 American Music Award, 3 Academy of Country Music Awards

Shelton's 2011 album *Red River Blue* became his first number one album. In 2012, he and Miranda performed at the Super Bowl. A year later, Shelton released his eighth album, *Based on a True Story. . .* It sold so many copies it went platinum.

Shelton and his wife, Miranda Lambert, pose with their Country Music Awards in 2012.

TAYLOR SWIFT SNAGS ALBUM OF THE YEAR AT AGE 20

Taylor Swift is one of country music's biggest stars. She grew up on her family's Christmas tree farm in Pennsylvania. Even as a child, Taylor loved to sing. By the time she was ten, she had sung at fairs and baseball games.

Swift moved to Nashville when she was 14. She insisted on writing and performing her own songs. She sang at the famous Bluebird Café. A record executive spotted her. He liked the young star. He offered her a record deal.

Swift released her debut album in 2006. The album was a success with more than just country fans. Fans of both country music and pop music loved it. In 2009, Swift became the first country artist to win an MTV Video Music Award. Then in 2010, she won four Grammys. They included Album of the Year for

1.2 million
Number of copies *Red* sold in its first week, the most of any album in a decade.

Full Name: Taylor Alison Swift

Birth Date: December 13, 1989

Birthplace: Reading, Pennsylvania

Breakthrough Moment: Swift's first single "Tim McGraw" became a top country hit in 2006.

Awards: 7 Grammy Awards, 15 American Music Awards

her record *Fearless*. In 2013, Swift became the youngest person to ever win Album of the Year. She was just 20 years old when she won it.

Swift is famous for writing songs about ex-boyfriends. Her millions of fans call themselves "Swifties." Swift has had 13 number one singles. She has sold millions of records.

Swift performs live in London in 2012.

JUSTIN TIMBERLAKE'S DEBUT SOLO ALBUM SELLS 7 MILLION COPIES

Justin Timberlake grew up singing in his church choir. He loved to entertain. He sang on the talent show *Star Search* when he was 11. It fueled his desire to perform. Timberlake joined the boy band 'N Sync when he was 14. The band sold millions of records.

In 2002, Timberlake went solo. His debut album sold more than 7 million copies around the world. Timberlake has worked with artists such as Madonna and Jay-Z. In 2005, he started his own record company called JayTee Records.

Timberlake has also acted in several movies. He has proven to be

Justin Timberlake performs in Brazil in 2013.

a funny comedian too. Timberlake has hosted the sketch comedy show *Saturday Night Live*. His performances earned two Emmys.

In 2012, Timberlake married actress Jessica Biel. He continues to write music. His 2013 album *The 20/20 Experience* sold almost 1 million copies in its first week.

5

Number of times through 2013 Timberlake has hosted *Saturday Night Live*.

Full Name: Justin Randall Timberlake

Birth Date: January 31, 1981

Birthplace: Memphis, Tennessee

Breakthrough Moment: Timberlake released his first solo album *Justified* in 2002.

Awards:
9 Grammy Awards, 3 Emmy Awards

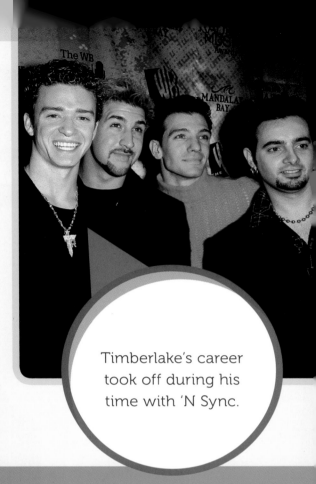

Timberlake's career took off during his time with 'N Sync.

MICKEY MOUSE CLUB

Timberlake got his start on the TV show *The New Mickey Mouse Club* in 1993. Timberlake and several of his castmates went on to become huge stars. The cast included Britney Spears, Christina Aguilera, Ryan Gosling, and JC Chasez. Timberlake and Chasez would later form the band 'N Sync.

PHARRELL WILLIAMS BREAKS AWAY WITH "HAPPY"

Pharrell Williams grew up listening to all sorts of music. He loved rock, pop, rap, and R&B. Pharrell joined his school band in the seventh grade. He played drums. His good friend, Chad Hugo, played saxophone. Pharrell and Chad experimented with different beats. They called themselves the Neptunes. In 1992, they sold their first song. They were still in high school. The Neptunes became known for their funky electronic sound. By 1998, music stars wanted to work with them.

Williams released his first solo album in 2006. It received mixed

Williams is known for wearing unique hats.

13

Number of countries in which "Blurred Lines" reached number one.

Full Name: Pharrell Williams

Birth Date: April 5, 1973

Birthplace: Virginia Beach, Virginia

Breakthrough Moment: In 2001, Williams helped produce top hits for Usher, Nelly, LL Cool J, and 'N Sync.

Awards: 7 Grammy Awards, 1 Academy Award nomination

Williams at the premiere of *Despicable Me 2* in 2013

reviews. Williams kept producing and working with other artists. He even worked with Madonna and Beyoncé.

Williams finally hit it big in 2013. He sang on two hit songs. These songs were Daft Punk's "Get Lucky" and Robin Thicke's "Blurred Lines." In November 2013, Williams released his smash hit "Happy" as part of the soundtrack to the movie *Despicable Me 2*. The song was nominated for an Oscar. In 2014, Williams earned seven Grammy nominations as a singer and producer. He won four Grammys.

Williams released his second album in 2014. Stars Justin Timberlake and Miley Cyrus sing on it. The album sold more than 100,000 copies in its first week.

FACT SHEET

- In 1958, *Billboard* magazine created its Hot 100 list. The Hot 100 is a list of the 100 most popular songs in a given week. The Hot 100 tracks any current song of any musical style. Songs are rated by how often they are played on the radio. They are also rated by sales. The Hot 100's formula has changed over time. In 2012, the magazine started tracking streaming services. Songs popular on Spotify or Pandora are now reflected in the Hot 100. In 2013, it started tracking YouTube plays.

- The first Grammy Awards were handed out in 1959. A group of record executives created the Grammys. They wanted to award the biggest talents in music. The original Grammys featured 28 categories. The 2014 Grammys had 82 categories. Grammys are awarded by the National Academy of Recording Arts and Sciences.

- The MP3 was born in July 1995. MP3s are digital music files. These files can be shared and transferred over the Internet. Before MP3s, music fans had to buy CDs, cassette tapes, or records. MP3s and iPods made music more accessible. They allow people to buy music from a computer or phone. Rihanna is the most successful digital musician. She has sold 120 million downloads of her songs.

- YouTube has launched many singers' careers. Pop star Justin Bieber got his start on YouTube. Bieber's mom posted videos of him singing to the website. Millions of viewers watched his performances. The videos caught the attention of record executives. Young pop star Greyson Chance has a similar story. Chance posted a video of himself performing a Lady Gaga song to YouTube. It received more than 52 million views. It helped earn Chance a record deal.

GLOSSARY

album
A collection of songs or recordings.

conservative
Traditional.

cover
A new performance of an old song or beat.

debut album
An artist or band's first album.

download
A song that has been copied into a computer or device.

Grammy Award
An honor given to talents in the music industry.

hip-hop
A type of music that involves rapping and rhythmic beats.

platinum
An album or single that has sold more than 1 million copies.

R&B
Short for rhythm and blues, R&B music combines soul, funk, pop, and hip-hop music.

record deal
A legal agreement between a record company and an artist.

single
A song released separately from an album.

FOR MORE INFORMATION

Books

Kaplan, Arie. *American Pop: Hit Makers, Superstars, and Dance Revolutionaries*. Minneapolis, MN: Twenty-First Century, 2013.

Landau, Elaine. *Beyoncé: R & B Superstar*. Minneapolis, MN: Lerner, 2013.

Napoli, Tony. *Justin Timberlake: Breakout Music Superstar*. Berkeley Heights, NJ: Enslow, 2010.

Websites

American Top 40
www.at40.com

Billboard's Hot 100
www.billboard.com/charts/hot-100

Grammy.com
www.grammy.com

INDEX

About the Author

Annabelle Tometich is an award-winning writer and reporter. She has written several children's books on topics ranging from lacrosse and gymnastics to nutrition and popular culture. Annabelle lives in Fort Myers, Florida, with her husband and their two really cute kids.

32

READ MORE FROM 12-STORY LIBRARY

Every 12-Story Library book is available in many formats, including Amazon Kindle and Apple iBooks. For more information, visit your device's store or 12StoryLibrary.com.